DE 13 '02	DATE DUE		
JA 24 '03			
DE 20 '04			
JA 11 '05			
MR 09 '05			
AP 01 '05			
FEB 2 5 '08			
MAR 1 0 '08			
APR 3 0 '09			

COSTUME, TRADITION, AND CULTURE:
REFLECTING ON THE PAST

Popular Superstitions

by

Mary Hughes

Chelsea House Publishers
Philadelphia

CHELSEA HOUSE PUBLISHERS
Editor-in-Chief Stephen Reginald
Managing Editor James D. Gallagher
Production Manager Pamela Loos
Art Director Sara Davis
Picture Editor Judy Hasday
Senior Production Editor Lisa Chippendale
Designer Takeshi Takahashi

3 5 7 9 8 6 4 2

Library of Congress Cataloging-in-Publication Data

Hughes, Mary.
Popular superstitions / by Mary Hughes.

    p. cm. — (Costume, tradition, and culture: reflecting on
the past)
Includes bibliographical references and index.
Summary: Explores twenty-five superstitions and how they
may have started, including those about walking under a ladder, breaking a mirror, and opening an umbrella indoors.

ISBN 0–7910–5172–2 (hardcover)
1. Superstition—Juvenile literature. [1. Superstition. 2. Folklore.] I. Title. II. Series.
BF1775.H87 1998   98–36081
398'.41—dc21   CIP
                                                     AC

CONTENTS

Introduction 4
About the Author 7
Overview: Popular Superstitions 8

Walking Under a Ladder 11
Falling of a Picture 13
Sneezing 15
Seeing the New Moon 17
A Howling Dog at Night 19
The Shoe at Weddings 21
Breaking a Mirror 23
Stumbling and Falling 25
Three Cigarettes, One Match 27
Burning of the Ear 29
The Banshee 31
The Mascot 33
Under the Mistletoe 35
The Lucky Spider 37
Spilling of Salt 39
Crossing a Knife and Fork 41
Whistling Up a Wind 43
Thirteen at Table 45
Shooting an Albatross 47
Lucky White Heather 49
Lucky Horseshoe 51
The Magpie 53
Putting on Left Shoe First 55
Umbrella Opened Indoors 57
The Raven 59

Chronology 60
Index 62
Further Reading 64

Introduction

For as long as people have known that other cultures existed, they have been curious about the differences in their customs and traditions. Julius Caesar, the famous Roman leader, wrote long chronicles about the inhabitants of Gaul (modern-day France) while he was leading troops in the Gallic Wars (58–51 B.C.). In the chronicles, he discussed their religious beliefs, their customs, their day-to-day life, and the conflicts among the different groups. Explorers like Marco Polo traveled thousands of miles and devoted years of their lives to learning about the peoples of the East and bringing home the stories of Chinese court life, along with the silks, spices, and inventions of that culture. The Chelsea House series *Costume, Tradition, and Culture: Reflecting on the Past* continues this legacy of exploration and discovery by discussing some of the most fascinating traditions, beliefs, legends, and artifacts from around the world.

Different cultures develop traditions and costumes to mark the roles of people in their societies, to commemorate events in their histories, and to make the changes and mysteries of life more meaningful. Soldiers wear uniforms to show that they are serving in their nation's army, and insignia on the uniforms show what ranks they hold within the army. People of Bukhara, a city in Uzbekistan, have for centuries woven fine threads of gold into their clothes, and when they travel to other cities they can be recognized as Bukharans by the golden embroidery on their traditional costume. For many years, in the Irish countryside, people would leave bowls of milk outside at night as an offering to the fairies, or "Good People," believing that this would help ensure their favor and keep the family safe from fairy mischief. In Mexico, November 2 is the Day of the Dead, when people visit cemeteries and have feasts to remember their ancestors. In the United States, brides wear white dresses, and the traditional wedding includes many rituals: the father of the bride "giving her away" to the groom, the exchange of vows and rings, the throwing of rice, the tossing of the bride's bouquet. These rituals and symbols help make the marriage meaningful and special for the couple, their families, and their friends, by expressing the change that is taking place and allowing the friends and families to wish luck to the couple.

This series will explore some of the myths, symbols, costumes, and traditions of various cultures from around the world and different times in the past. *Fighting Units of the American War of Independence,* for example, will detail the uniforms, weapons, and decorations of the regiments and battalions on both sides of the war, along with the battles in which they became famous. *Roman Myths, Heroes, and Legends* describes how the ancient Romans explained the wonders and natural phenomena of their world with fantastic stories of superhuman heroes and almost human deities who could change the course of history at will. In *Popular Superstitions,* you will learn how some familiar superstitious beliefs—such as throwing spilled salt over your shoulder, or hanging a horseshoe over your door for good luck—originally began, in times when people feared that devils and evil spirits were meddling in their lives. Few people still believe in malicious spirits, but many still toss the spilled salt over their shoulders, or knock on wood when expressing cautious hope. The legendary figures of a culture—the brave explorers of *The Wild West* or the wicked brigands described in *Infamous Pirates*—help shape that culture's values by providing grand, almost mythical examples of what people should (or should not!) strive to be.

The illustrations that accompany these books have their own cultural history. Originally, they were printed on small collectors' cards and sold in the early 20th century. Each card in a set of 25 or 50 would depict a different person, artifact, or event, and usually the reverse side would offer a few sentences of description to explain the picture. Now, they provide a fascinating glimpse into history and an entertaining addition to the stories presented here.

ABOUT THE AUTHOR

MARY HUGHES graduated from the University of Maryland with a degree in Radio, Television, and Film. She enjoyed substitute teaching for many years before tackling her current assignment as a computer lab technician at an elementary school in Maryland. An avid baseball fan, she writes feature articles about ballplayers in the Baltimore Orioles organization. She often gets an inside peek at just what it takes to make it to the big leagues. She's well aware that while some superstition exists in baseball, its impact on the game will always be superseded by skill. Her favorite ballplayer is her teenage son, Mark Hudson.

Overview
Popular Superstitions

Former Baltimore Orioles pitcher Jim Palmer ate pancakes all the way to baseball's Hall of Fame. On the days he was scheduled to pitch, Palmer confesses, "I had to have 'cakes for breakfast." Veteran reliever Norm Charlton has been known to trash a clubhouse following a particularly bad outing, but he is quick to add, "I have never broken a mirror. Never."

It's amazing to think that a present-day ballplayer subscribes to a superstition that's probably older than mirrors themselves. Why is that? How did such ancient superstitions get started in the first place, and why have they managed to survive centuries later?

The word superstition itself comes from the Latin, *superstes,* which means "outliving or surviving." Superstition has been defined as a "belief in a sign of things to come" and as the "outward manifestations of deep-seated anxieties." However silly or serious they may seem, all superstitions are said to "have a dual purpose: to attract favorable influences and to ward off unfavorable ones." Eric Maple writes, "Superstition is a form of personal magic which is used for the purpose of coming to terms with the unknown."

Not all ballplayers are superstitious. Orioles center fielder Brady Anderson claims he is "the perfect example of someone who's not the least bit superstitious." Brady's pre-game and postgame workouts are designed to prepare him for the game of baseball, period.

Sitting in the visitor's dugout with his arms crossed in his lap and his legs crossed at the ankles, Texas Rangers manager Johnny Oates smiles. "I'd like to think I'm not superstitious," he says. Then, in case anyone has missed all of the crossing, Oates laughs and crosses his eyes.

WALKING UNDER A LADDER

When a saying or a superstition gets passed down through time, it sometimes loses something in translation. This may help explain the widely held superstition that walking under a ladder is unlucky. Though this particular superstition is fairly new compared to those that originated with the caveman, it is, nevertheless, steeped in history, dating back to the 1700s.

In those days, public hanging was the execution of choice for those convicted of a serious crime. Gallows were constructed to accommodate the criminals to be executed, but the exact height of each person to be hanged had to be taken into consideration, which required last-minute adjustments to the length of the rope.

The rope had to be just short enough to allow the feet of the person to be hanged to completely clear the floor below. This way, the person's weight dropping suddenly and dangling from the noose without support from below would be enough to break the neck (or, if the criminal was unlucky enough not to break his neck, he would strangle).

The executioners leaned a ladder against the top cross beam of the gibbet, as shown in the picture, so that they could climb up to tie off the rope, knotting it to hang at the appropriate length.

Waiting below, beneath the ladder, was the person about to be executed. Hence, it became "unlucky to walk under a ladder," as this meant almost certain death was imminent, since the doomed man was "almost at the end of his rope."

FALLING OF A PICTURE

In some instances, superstitions were based on what is known as "sympathetic magic," in which "like produces like." The caveman practiced sympathetic magic by visualizing what would happen during the tribe's upcoming hunt for food.

By drawing trapped or speared animals on the cave walls, the cave artist was willing his tribe's hunters to recreate during their actual hunt the scene depicted on the wall. The artist believed this would happen because he subscribed to the theory that like produces like.

In more recent times, following the invention of the photograph, cultures unfamiliar with cameras still sometimes fear that the photographer will "steal their souls"—that the life force of the persons photographed will be pulled from them and held captive in the camera or the resulting picture.

In our society, with the introduction of lifelike formal portraits, it came to be believed that if something happened to a person's picture, the same thing would happen to the actual person. So, if a man's picture were to be hung upside down, the man himself, like the picture, would feel disoriented. When a picture fell, it foretold the death of the person in the picture.

Some people thought that to turn a person's photograph over in a frame, so as to be unable to see their face, was most unlucky. During the 1700s there was even a custom that had a man stare into a mirror until he had "frozen" his image within the mirror, so that it would not disappear. He then would give the mirror to the woman he wished to marry. Tradition held that if the lady smiled, she liked the man, but if she turned the mirror over, she did not.

SNEEZING

Simply by uttering the words "God bless you" at the sound of a sneeze, people who would hardly consider themselves superstitious may be perpetuating one of the most widespread superstitions of all. Like a smile, or a laugh, the sneeze knows no international boundaries.

Not only is its own sound universal, but so, it would seem, is the verbal response a sneeze elicits from those who hear it. Germans respond by saying, "Gesunheit," the Zulu say, "I am now blessed," and the English utter, "Bless you." When a Hindu sneezes, he is told to "Live" and responds by saying, "With you." Greeks and Romans were heard to say, "Banish the omen," on hearing a sneeze.

Why all the precautionary blessing and banning? An outward symptom of several illnesses—even plagues—the sneeze has been labeled sinister and supernatural by many different cultures because it is an involuntary physical phenomenon: The heart stops beating momentarily, as air is suddenly and noisily expelled.

According to legend, a sneeze symbolized the expulsion of the breath of life from the body. It followed then, that if a person were to lose his or her soul by sneezing, a demon could easily enter this body without a soul through any opening.

A sneezing Brahmin in India makes sure to touch his ears to keep spirits from entering through them. Natives of the Celebes Islands forced fishhooks through their nostrils to prevent this invasion of evil. In China, plugging nostrils with pieces of jade served the same purpose.

SEEING THE NEW MOON

The superstitions dictating how one should observe the new moon—the first phase of the moon, when it appears as a slim crescent—tended to be quite detailed. For instance, in keeping with the notion that it was unlucky to view the new moon from indoors, it was believed that it was unlucky to see the new moon through glass.

However, because poor eyesight required many people to wear eyeglasses, the superstition was amended to make an exception for spectacles, making it acceptable to watch the moon through one's glasses.

It was considered unlucky to point at the moon at any time. One would do better to bow to all new moons, especially if the new moon happened to be the first new moon of a new year.

At the first sight of a new moon, it was advisable to make a wish, and for an extra bit of luck, one should turn a silver coin in one's pocket or purse while making the wish. This was thought to bring good fortune and wealth that would grow along with the moon. A wish made on a new moon wouldn't work if it were made through a closed window, as something was sure to come between the wishing person and the good luck he or she sought.

If the new moon was sighted on a person's right, or straight ahead, it was considered lucky. If it was spotted on the left, or behind the superstitiuous person, bad luck was in store for the weeks ahead.

A HOWLING DOG AT NIGHT

ncient humans did their best to explain the world around them. They believed that dogs possessed supernatural perceptions, because dogs could hear and smell things that humans could not. When the caveman heard a dog howling incessantly, he took that to mean that the angel of death was close by. Why else would man's best friend be barking nonstop?

In the early civilization of Egypt it was also believed that dogs, being familiar with the world beyond the grave, could detect the presence of spirits and ghosts. Egyptians worshiped dogs; they named the brightest star in the sky Sirius, the Dog Star, and they used this star to predict droughts and floods.

In many civilizations, it was thought that the gateway to hell was guarded by a dog. The Greek named the monstrous watchdog of the underworld Cerberus. Sporting three dog heads, a serpent for a tail, and lots of snakes' heads on his back, Cerberus had the job of keeping the living out of the realm of the dead, as well as preventing the occupants of Hades from leaving.

The Hindus believed that the demons that would enter the corpses of the dead when the souls had departed could only be expelled by the glance of a dog with four eyes or, lacking that, a dog with two spots over his eyes.

Early Persians held that the fierce barking of a yellow-eared, four-eyed dog would drive the devil from the souls of the holy ones as they walked across the bridge into eternity.

THE SHOE AT WEDDINGS

Following the wedding ceremony and reception, most newlywed couples take a honeymoon trip. Traditionally, the other members of the wedding party decorate the car in which the bride and groom will set off to begin their new life together.

Custom dictates that a pair of shoes be tied to the rear of the couple's vehicle—a reminder of the old practice of the bride's father giving her shoe to her new husband. Perhaps this tie between footwear and marriage explains something of the fairy tale of Cinderella, Prince Charming, and the glass slipper, with its many variants throughout Europe.

Not just shoes but also stockings have found their way into wedding traditions. In Western Europe 300 years ago, long before cars and honeymoon trips, the newly married couple and their entire wedding party danced their way to what was to become the home of the bride and groom. The bride's mother would be there, ready to say her goodbyes to her daughter and new son-in-law.

With their wedding party surrounding them, the new husband and wife sat up in bed in their wedding clothes, while each bridesmaid got a chance to throw the bridegroom's stocking over her shoulder, taking aim at the groom and hoping to hit him in the face.

Next, the groom's men took turns tossing the bride's stocking over their shoulders, each one striving to hit the bride in the face. Supposedly, anyone who was able to hit the mark would soon marry. Today's wedding superstition dictates that the groom throw his bride's garter and the bride toss her bouquet to determine who in their party will be the next to marry.

BREAKING A MIRROR

irrors have long provided humans with a chance to reflect. Early humans thought the image reflected in the water was that of their souls, which they believed could exist apart from the body. They feared that evil spirits lurking in the water could snatch their souls, dragging them deep into the netherworld below.

Fascinated at seeing their own reflections, humans soon found ways to improve on the watery images that nature provided by creating manmade mirrors. The early Greeks, Romans, and Egyptians fashioned mirrors from bronze and silver. By the early 1200s, the people of Venice had devised the more modern—and less costly—method of making mirrors from glass.

Mirrors and myths have been intertwined throughout history. The Chinese hung mirrors with the hope that evil spirits would be scared off at the sight of their own reflections. Queen Elizabeth of England had a mirror designed to deflect the evil eye. Legend has it that anyone staring into a mirror too long will see the devil.

The Greeks told of young Narcissus, who was so taken at the beauty of his own reflection in a fountain that he could not bear to look away. He died, becoming a frozen statue to self-love, a warning to all who would become too self-involved.

Breaking a mirror is said to bring seven years of bad luck. However, it is also said that the curse can be broken by either burying the broken pieces or by throwing the shards into a stream flowing south.

STUMBLING AND FALLING

I n the theater, stumbling is good or bad, depending on one's point of view. There are those who believe that it's good luck to trip while making an entrance on stage, getting any bad luck over and done with right away. Others are of the opinion that stumbling means that one of the actors will soon either miss a cue or forget a line.

All are in agreement, however, that it's best to avoid wishing each other good luck prior to the curtain going up, for that would tempt fate. Instead, it's universally accepted in show business that performers be told to "Break a leg." Perhaps gaining, rather than losing, something in the translation, it is traditional to say to Germany's opera performers, "*Hals und Beinbruch,*" or "Break your neck *and* legs!"

Some believe that evil spirits live on doorsteps. These spirits cause people to stumble on their way out of their homes. For some, this serves as a warning that they are ill-advised to go any farther.

Some modern-day specialists in human behavior suggest that stumbling can be unconsciously self-induced. If a person stumbles, there may be something causing him or her not to want to go forward—a person, place, or situation to be avoided.

Because an evil spirit might cause a bride to stumble as she enters her new home for the first time as a wife, it has long been customary for the bridegroom to carry his bride across the threshold.

THREE CIGARETTES, ONE MATCH

It's usually impossible to trace a saying directly back to any one person or persons who introduced it to the world of superstition. However, in the case of the expression, "Three on a match must never be," it is entirely possible, making the surrounding set of circumstances somewhat suspicious.

Matches were invented during the 1800s, and by the early 1900s the world's supply had come to be controlled by a man who became known as the "Swedish Match King." Ivar Kreuger was an enterprising Swede who naturally wanted to see his business venture do well. It's not surprising then that Kreuger would want to sell as many matches as possible.

It seems highly likely that Kreuger took advantage of two war-time situations of the period to advance his cause by popularizing the romantic story that letting a match flicker long enough to light three cigarettes had endangered the lives of those encamped in the trenches. If that is indeed the case, Kreuger may have been one of the earliest advertisers to "match" his market to his customer.

The South African War, sometimes known as the Boer War, was fought from 1899 to 1902. A dozen years later, World War I erupted in Europe. Both wars were characterized by the use of trenches, ditches dug deep enough to afford an army's men protection from enemy sight and guns. Kreuger's story undoubtedly made it seem foolish for soldiers to keep a match lit for long, as it could prove a fatal mistake.

BURNING OF THE EAR

Pliny, an early Roman naturalist, was quite a prolific author. He wrote of using hazel wands to divine underground springs, of preventing marital woes by rubbing wolf fat on the threshold of the wedding chamber, and of how spittle had proven effective in curing boils, eye infections, epilepsy, and leprosy. Not surprisingly, his critics accused him of not separating fact from fiction in his writings.

Born Gaius Plinius Caecilius Secundus in northern Italy in A.D. 23 or 24, Pliny practiced law and served as both a Roman official and a cavalryman in the Roman legions. His 37 volume *Natural History* has been called one of the most important works of classical Latin literature, because he took great pains to record the stories, myths, and beliefs of his day.

Because his writings have endured, he has provided modern society with a glimpse into a world long gone. Pliny died in the year 79, on August 24, as he attempted to record an account of the eruption of Mt. Vesuvius at Pompeii. The poisonous fumes overcame him.

Attempting to base theory in scientific fact, Pliny tried to make some sense of something he had heard or read that suggested one's ear would burn when someone else was talking about them. He suggested the existence of universal sounds waves conducted by mercury that could travel great distances.

Pliny wound up slightly off base, as did those who further speculated that when the right ear burns, something nice was being said, when it's the left, something ill.

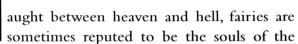# THE BANSHEE

aught between heaven and hell, fairies are sometimes reputed to be the souls of the unfortunate pagan dead who were left to die without having been baptized. Not deliberately evil enough for hell yet not quite good enough to be allowed into heaven, it is the fairy's fate to wander the netherworld in between.

Fairies have also been described as the fallen angels who were cast out of heaven following the revolt of Lucifer against God. It is said they were spared the agony of hell when God raised His hand to stop them in midflight, condemning them to remain wherever they happened to be at the time—be it in the air, on land, or in the water.

More likely, fairies are remnants of the pagan spirits of trees and streams, the "elementals" recognized by tribal cultures throughout the world. They played a major role in the pre-Christian, Druidic religion of the British Isles.

In Ireland and the Western Highlands of Scotland, a particular fairy, known as "the woman of the fairies," permeates local folklore with her trademark wails and screams. Americanized to "banshee," the Irish spelling is *bean sidhe*.

Legend has it that when the woman of the fairies can be heard wailing in the night, death will soon visit the family hearing her cries. However, many believe that the cries of the banshee are none other than those of a nearby owl.

Regarded as a symbol of death and mourning since the days of early Egypt, the owl's cries have frightened the superstitious for centuries. Owls, with their nocturnal habits, sounding at times like a dreadfully despondent human being, have also long been linked with witchcraft.

THE MASCOT

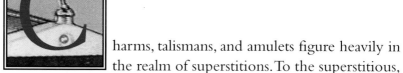

harms, talismans, and amulets figure heavily in the realm of superstitions. To the superstitious, they represent good luck or offer protection from harm. Some amulets were designed to be worn or carried by the person needing their help.

Someone stricken by a disease might be given a necklace made from a walnut shell. The shell might contain a spider wrapped in silk, which was believed to cure any number of illnesses. Other amulets were designed to be carried by the infirm or those desiring strength and power. Still other amulets, such as the iron horseshoe, were intended to be mounted on a building or bedpost to provide protection from evil spirits, witches, or demons of the night.

From the scarabs favored by the early Egyptians to the Islamic blue beads said to ward off the evil eye, there have been multitudes of amulets, including stones, bones, coins, medallions, insects, and the rabbit's foot. Religions may dictate the belief in certain amulets. Other charms are chosen based solely on the bearer's particular beliefs.

The mascots adopted by schools and colleges, athletic teams, and political associations of recent times are descended from these early symbols of good fortune. In the United States, the donkey is the mascot of the Democratic Party, and the Republican Party's mascot is the elephant.

Hood ornaments on cars and trucks easily identify their particular maker. And sports fans spend millions of dollars each year on merchandise sporting their favorite team's colors, logo, and mascot.

UNDER THE MISTLETOE

ncient people thought mistletoe to be magical for several reasons. Its berries are white, the most pure and sacred of all colors. Its leaves remain evergreen, full of life, even in the midst of winter when most trees are bare. And, mystically, mistletoe thrives high in the treetops, far from the earthly soil below.

Scientists now know that mistletoe is a parasite and that its seeds are spread by birds. Sprouting in the bark of trees, mistletoe needs to penetrate the outer cover of its host plant with its woody rootlike sinkers in order to survive.

Early Roman author Pliny (Gaius Plinius Secundus) described a Druid mistletoe harvest as a religious ceremony taking place on the sixth day of the moon in an oak grove. A priest wearing a white robe would climb an oak and cut the mistletoe with his left hand, using a bronze sickle gilded with gold. The mistletoe was caught in a white cloth, so as to keep it from touching the ground.

The ceremony was not complete until two white bulls were sacrificed and a feast held. The mistletoe would then offer protection against the devil, witchcraft, and evil. Its medicinal powers were thought to be all-healing, and it was given to calm epileptic seizures. (For a more humorous view of Druids and mistletoe, pick up a copy of the *Asterix* comic book, produced in Europe, about a small town in ancient Gaul that held off the Romans.)

It was believed that a woman kissed beneath mistletoe would bear children because the berries symbolized fertility. Throughout the centuries mistletoe hanging overhead has been an invitation to those standing below it to kiss.

THE LUCKY SPIDER

he English have a saying, "If you would live and thrive, let a spider run alive." They consider it unlucky to kill a spider, for that may cause a thunderstorm. Many Tahitians also won't harm spiders, as they believe them to be the shadows of gods.

According to folk magic, eating a black spider between two slices of buttered bread every morning gives one great power and strength. Eating a spider wrapped in raisins or butter was often prescribed as a cure for whooping cough.

Some who drew the line at eating spiders liked to place them in amulets, wearing them about their necks to ward off disease. An effective amulet could be fashioned by wrapping one to three spiders in silk and placing them in a walnut shell.

The rule of thumb was this: if there's time to bake a spider beforehand, only one is required; otherwise, three are necessary. A spider amulet was especially popular as a cure for the ague, a dreadful combination of chills and fevers. Lacking a spider, their webs have been used to cure both the ague and warts.

The webs that spiders weave have been linked to creativity, imagination, destiny, and the waxing and waning of the moon. If a spiderweb falls inexplicably, according to one old Hebrew superstition, a flood is on its way.

In some cultures letting a specific spider crawl over you will bring riches. In England, it is the golden spider that hints of coming wealth; in the Ozark mountains of the United States, it is the red spider.

SPILLING OF SALT

Italian Renaissance artist Leonardo da Vinci illustrated a friendship about to be broken in his famous painting *The Last Supper* by depicting renegade apostle Judas as having upset the saltcellar. Eating another man's salt created a sacred bond; spilling it broke that bond and the friendship, and threatened the spirit of health.

Salt was highly regarded in ancient civilizations. Essential to the diet and a natural preservative for food, it represented life and incorruptibility, the symbolic enemy of decay. The Latin word, *salarium,* meaning "salt allowance," is the root of the modern word "salary." Indeed, Roman laborers and soldiers were paid partly in salt.

According to Finnish folklore, the sky god Ukko sent a spark of fire from the heavens into the sea, which turned to salt. Many fishermen sprinkled their nets with salt to protect their boat and its crew; others did so as an offering to the gods of the sea. Salt was typically placed between the planks of a ship as it was being built for the same reasons (and perhaps too to symbolically prevent rotting of the wood).

In Ireland, brides and grooms were given a plate of oatmeal and salt, while in the United States, bread and salt were bestowed on new homeowners to ensure their happiness. In many cultures, on the first visit to a new home it was customary to put salt in a child's mouth.

It was also believed that a pinch of salt in a baby's cradle would protect the babe from evil until its baptism, and that salt thrown over the left shoulder would fly straight into the devil's face. Those who accidentally spilled salt, then, could ward off bad luck by tossing a few grains over their shoulder.

CROSSING A KNIFE AND FORK

E tiquette dictates that a table be set with forks to the left and knives and spoons to the right of the dinner plate. This makes it easy for the diner to reach for a fork with his left hand in order to pierce his food while cutting it with the knife held in his right.

A crossover takes place when the knife is placed on the plate and the fork is transferred to the right hand so the food can be brought to the mouth. This crisscrossing continues throughout the meal. This custom is more prevalent in America than elsewhere. In most parts of Europe diners don't bother transferring the fork to the right hand.

The cross is one of the most important and universal symbols in the world. To Christians, it stands for the holy cross on which Christ died. In the mythology of Scandinavia, Thor, the god of thunder, had a cross-shaped hammer.

Farmers first placed crosses in their fields to ward off evil spirits. As time went on, attempts were made to disguise the cross by adding clothes. According to one theory, this is how the modern-day scarecrow evolved, although the belief today is that the scarecrow's resemblance to a human figure scares away the crows.

Crossing one's fingers, which once had to do with scaring off the devil, has come to mean that a wish will come true. This happens, supposedly, because the wish gets trapped between the crossed fingers. On the other hand, crossing one's fingers during the making of a promise can negate the promise.

WHISTLING UP A WIND

Superstitious sailors frown on whistling while at sea, because to do so is said to imitate the wind, which could provoke a storm. Whistling softly is thought to induce a breeze, but an out-and-out gale will blow up if the whistling is too loud.

Some believe it is better to throw a pack of playing cards overboard to command a fair wind than to risk a storm by whistling too loudly. Some believe favorable winds can also be brought about by a sneeze made over the ship's starboard side.

Whistling is the subject of superstition on dry land as well. It is said that callous women whistled while the workmen were forging the nails that were to be used for Christ's cross.

It's considered extremely bad luck to whistle anywhere in a theater, particularly in a dressing room, because whistling foretells that someone will soon be unemployed. Superstitious actors subscribe to the notion that they will be given two weeks' notice if someone whistles in their dressing room.

In the event that a dressing room is shared, it is thought that the soon-to-be-unemployed actor is the one nearest the door. If the whistler also happens to be an actor, the spell can be reversed, but only if the offending whistler is immediately sent out of the theater and turns around three times outside before returning to the room.

In the world of horse racing, many jockeys consider whistling unlucky and forbid it in the paddock before a race.

THIRTEEN AT TABLE

Jesus Christ died on the cross the day following the Last Supper, at which there were 13 at the table. This probably prompted the belief that it was bad luck to have 13 at a table and that death would visit someone who had been seated at that table within the year.

According to a Scandinavian legend, 12 gods planning to have a feast did not invite Loki, the god of mischief. Unfortunately, Loki got wind of the feast, became angry at having not been included on the guest list, and decided to attend the dinner even though he was well aware that he hadn't been invited. At the feast, he convinced a blind god, Hoder, to kill another guest. Hoder shot Balder, the god of goodness, with an arrow made of mistletoe.

The number 13 is generally considered unlucky by the superstitious. For this reason, many theaters attempt to conceal where row 13 is located. That is why rows are given letters, instead of numbers, with the first two rows purposely being designated as AA and BB, prior to row A, in order to make it hard to detect which row in the theater is actually the 13th.

Actors about to begin rehearsal on a new production will ask an extra person to sit in on their first read through if the total of people at the table including the director, actors, and actresses would otherwise be 13.

Many skyscrapers, especially those built early in the twentieth century, have no official 13th floor. They skip from 12 to 14.

Historically, Hindus may have been the first to believe that 13 people sitting together was unlucky.

SHOOTING AN ALBATROSS

An albatross is an enormous seabird, clumsy on land but remarkably aerodynamic in flight. Its wings are extremely long, giving the bird an incredible wingspan of 10 to 12 feet. Though long, the wings are streamlined for flight, with a width of only about nine inches. The wings of the albatross are tailor-made for long flights, allowing the bird to stay aloft for extended periods while expending little effort.

According to legend, the albatross brings wind and fog to the sea. Although the wind may be desirable at some times, at other times it is not, making the presence of the albatross unwanted. Naturally, fog can create dangerous situations at sea, making navigation difficult at best, leaving the fog-inducing albatross to be regarded as a serious nuisance.

But, as the picture and its caption explain, there's always a risk involved if one kills an albatross, as there's a possibility that the bird is the reincarnation of a sailor who's been lost at sea.

Many sailors subscribed to the theory that certain birds, especially gulls, petrels, and the albatross, were doomed to wander the skies aimlessly, endlessly circling ships at sea, because they contained the souls of dead sailors.

In 1798 the English poet Samuel Taylor Coleridge wrote *Rime of the Ancient Mariner*, in which a mariner kills an albatross and has it hung around his neck for penance. Coleridge insisted that the entire poem was pure imagination. However, his story so well suited the superstitious sailors who had long believed the birds to be haunted that they accepted it to be true, and it has served to perpetuate the myth ever since.

LUCKY WHITE HEATHER

Just as the Native American was careful to use every part of the buffalo, eating its meat and fashioning garments and moccasins from its hide, so the Inuit, or American Eskimo, resourcefully put every bit of the whale to good use, from its blubber to its bones.

In much the same way, people throughout Great Britain, Europe, and parts of Africa have made the most of their bounty—an abundance of flowering heather growing on the moors of their homelands. There are over 600 varieties of the low-growing evergreen shrub, which is also known as heath, and almost as many uses for the prolific plants.

Brushes and brooms are made from heather throughout Europe, and baskets are fashioned from its trailing shoots. In France, the roots of the briarwood heather are used to make pipes for smoking. In Scotland the people create their thatched roofs from the heather that grows on the moors nearby.

The liquid made from heather is used in the tanning of leather. Some of the young heather shoots are fed to the domesticated animals on farms, and many birds favor eating the seeds of the plant. Because peat has long been a fuel source in many European countries, the fact that heather comprises a good deal of the material that fills the peat bogs makes it an important and valuable commodity.

The music and folklore of Scotland is filled with references to heath's colorful blossoms, known as heather bells. Only rarely were the long clusters of wild heather bells white, so these came to be known as lucky.

LUCKY HORSESHOE

A blacksmith of noble birth, St. Dunstan is reported to have outsmarted the devil, who came into his forge requesting to be shod. Dunstan knew the hoofed, two-legged creature to be the devil and made sure to drive the nails into his feet with extra force. This caused the devil to flee in pain, vowing never to enter a house with a horseshoe hung over its door again.

In the realm of folklore, a horseshoe is so versatile that it might "behoove" the superstitious to stock up on the iron equestrian charms in order to be ready for anything. Today most people simply regard the horseshoe as a symbol of good luck. For best results, they hang the talisman with the curve at the base and the two edges pointing upward, so luck will not run out.

In earlier times, however, the superstitious commonly hung the U-shaped charm upside down to ward off witches, fairies, the evil eye, and evil spirits, as well as the devil himself. Anyone wanting to accomplish both of these goals would need at least two horseshoes, because legend has it that once a horseshoe is in place, it must never be removed, lest it lose its effectiveness.

A third horseshoe becomes necessary for anyone wanting to place one on their chimney top to prevent witches from flying in on their broomsticks.

Anyone desiring to repel nightmares and other demons of the night will require a fourth horseshoe for nailing to their bedpost.

THE MAGPIE

Colored as it is with both black, the color associated with evil, and white—the purest and most sacred of all colors—the magpie is puzzling to the superstitious. Some say the magpie is a cross between the raven and the dove that Noah released from the Ark.

The magpie is related to crows and jays. It is one of the larger birds to be found in Great Britain and creates a sizable nest from sticks. The magpie's dwelling features a unique side entrance.

Kept as pets, the birds have been known to mimic words. Some Swedes maintain that there's a drop of Satan's blood on the magpie's tongue, thereby affording it human speech. Long the stuff of folklore, poems, and songs, magpies have been used to predict what the future holds in store for those who see them flying overhead.

All one needs to do is count the number of magpies and then listen to a poem that explains what that particular number of birds means. The poem accompanying the picture is but one variation on a theme. Here's another:

One for sorrow, two for joy,
Three for a girl, four for a boy.

Some Germans believed a singing magpie near a home foretold disaster, while a chattering magpie meant a guest was coming to visit. German folklore also told of witches riding on the backs of magpies.

Tipping your hat to a magpie was customary in Wales, and in England it was considered good luck to make a wish on the first magpie of spring.

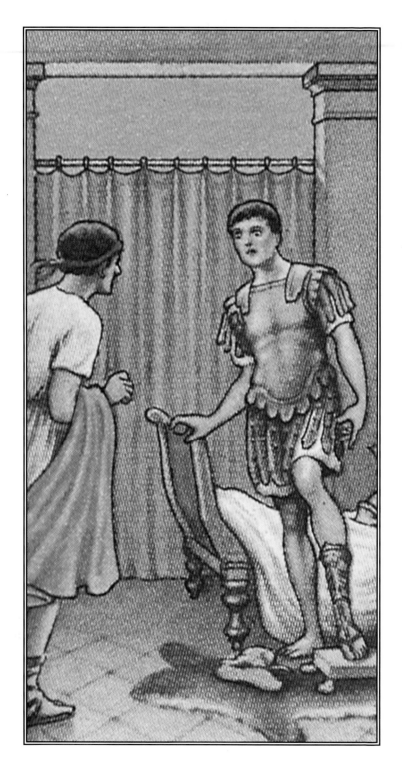

PUTTING ON LEFT SHOE FIRST

his superstition conjures up all sorts of left-right issues. The word "right" has come to mean correct, while the word "left" carries many negative connotations. (Interestingly, the numbers to the right of zero on the number line are positive; those to the left are negative.)

The French word for left is *gauche,* which also means clumsy, awkward, or "out of true." For many years parents and educators forced left-handers to stop using the "wrong" hand, making them use their right hand for writing. A person who has made this change is said to be "dextrosinistral," a word that sounds rather foreboding.

"Dextro" means right-handed, and "sinistral" means left-handed, unlucky, fraudulent, evil, and of ill-omen by means of being on the left. And "ambidextrous," the term for those lucky people who can use either hand equally well, really means "both right hands."

However, the human heart is on the left side of the body, and because the heart symbolizes love, engagement and wedding rings are traditionally worn on the left hand.

As for Caesar's sandals, scientific tests have shown that people, being creatures of habit, tend to always put on the same shoe first, regardless of which shoe that may be.

Those who are right-handed will generally put on their right shoe first, and left-handers will usually put on their left shoe before their right. Most people are unaware of their own preference but become uncomfortable when they do things differently. Because Augustus Caesar was accustomed to donning his right sandal first and inadvertently reversed his usual routine, he probably felt something was wrong.

UMBRELLA OPENED INDOORS

mbrellas, which first appeared thousands of years ago in Asia and along the Mediterranean, were more often used as sunshades than as protection from rain. Hence, those who worshipped the sun were wary of opening an umbrella indoors, because that might insult the power and spirit of the sun.

Though umbrellas largely disappeared from Europe following the collapse of the Roman Empire, they reappeared in more complex forms starting in the 16th century—again, mainly to shield the holder from the sun.

In more modern times, some believed that to open an umbrella inside was to invite rain and other misfortunes to enter the home. They also maintained that an open umbrella inside a building showed a lack of respect for the roof that had been designed for protection from the elements.

Some seafarers think it unlucky to have an umbrella on board a ship, probably believing it could invite a storm. And considering the close quarters of most vessels, an open umbrella, with its many sharp points, could prove physically dangerous.

This was clearly the case in Europe, where early umbrellas opened rather suddenly and clumsily. People were liable to be hurt, and objects in the path of the umbrella's swift opening stood a good chance of being broken.

Common sense suggests that a hostess receiving a guest who's just come in from the rain would rather keep a dripping umbrella away from her floors, carpeting, and furniture. For this reason, umbrella stands are placed in many foyers and entry halls as a designated place for a visitor's wet umbrella.

THE RAVEN

E dgar Allan Poe's poem "The Raven" did nothing to improve the reputation of this black bird. The annoying repetitiveness of Poe's verse reminded his readers of the bird's noisy, incessant cawing.

For hundreds of years, that cawing has been associated with evil. The largest member of the crow family, the raven is a deep glossy black. Its coloring alone gives rise to numerous superstitions, as black is associated with death, the devil, and the depths of hell. Indeed, many people believed that to see such a bird fly over their house during the evening meant that Death would soon visit their doorstep.

Early Romans believed that kicking a crow in the morning scared away demons. In ancient Athens it was thought that anyone eating the raw hearts of three crows would be able to predict the future. Later, in Czechoslovakia, that same meal came to mean that the diner would become a sharpshooter.

Washing one's hair with crows' eggs in ancient Greece was thought to dye gray hair black, but those who desired such results were warned to fill their mouths with oil during the hair washing or else their teeth would also turn black. Babylonians believed that sadness was sure to come to anyone dreaming of a crow cawing.

Much negativity surrounds the raven's eating habits. It eats the eggs of other birds and the young of other animals, as well as carrion—dead and putrefying flesh.

A warily intelligent bird, the raven can eerily mimic human speech, making it ideal for Poe's purposes in his poem.

Chronology

30,000 B.C.	Paleolithic art in caves depicted hunting, on the theory that "like produces like."
12,000 B.C.	Early humans domesticate dogs, which howl at night.
4000 B.C.	Egyptians depict the owl as a symbol of death and place spiders in amulets; sunshades (umbrellas) flourish in Asia and the Mediterranean.
1000 B.C.	The biblical tale of the Flood gives rise to superstitions about the raven and the magpie.
500 B.C.	Rome becomes a republic; British Druids harvest mistletoe and call white the sacred color.
A.D. 14	Augustus Caesar dies knowing he should have put his right sandal on first.
23-79	Pliny records whistling up the wind and burning of the ear legends.
30-100	At the Last Supper, 13 at a table becomes unlucky for dining; the Christian cross becomes a symbol of suffering and redemption.
600	The father of an Anglo-Saxon bride gives her shoe to the groom to touch to his forehead.
909	St. Dunstan born; he later shoes the devil.
1028-1085	William the Conqueror stumbles at Bulverhyte but saves face before his men.

1581   Public hangings begin at Tyburn.

c. 1600   Archbishop Laud learns that his picture has fallen, a sign that he will soon die.

1798   Samuel Taylor Coleridge writes "Ryme of the Ancient Mariner" in which a killed albatross brings bad luck.

1899   Ivar Kreuger, the Swedish Match King, popularizes the idea that three users of a match in battle are too many, a claim he repeats in 1912.

INDEX ☉

Albatross, 47
Amulets, 33, 37
Anderson, Brady, 8
Angels, fallen, 31
Augustus Caesar, 55

Babylonians, 59
Balder, 45
Ballplayers, 8–9
Banshee, 31
Blessings, after sneezing, 15
Boer War, 27
"Break a leg," 25
Breaking a mirror, 23

Cave art, 13
Celebes Islanders, 15
Cerberus, 19
Charlton, Norm, 8
Charms, 33
China, 15, 23
Cinderella story, 21
Coleridge, Samuel Taylor, 47
Crosses and crossing, 41
Czechoslovakia, 59

Dogs, 19
Doorsteps, 25
Druids, mistletoe and, 35

Ear, burning of, 29
England, 23, 37, 53

Fairies, 31
Fallen angels, 31
Falling, 25
  of picture, 13
Fingers, crossing, 41
Finns, 39
Fork, crossing with knife, 41

Germans, 53
Greeks, ancient, 15, 19, 23, 59

Hangings, 11
Heather, 49
Hindus, 19, 45
Horse racing, 43
Horseshoes, 51
Howling dog at night, 19

India, 15
Ireland, 31, 39

Knife and fork, crossing, 41
Kreuger, Ivar, 27

Ladder, walking under, 11
Last Supper, 45
Last Supper, The (Leonardo), 39
Left-right superstitions, 55
Leonardo da Vinci, 39
Loki, 45
Lucky horseshoe, 51
Lucky white heather, 49

Magpie, 53
Mascots, 33
Matches, 27
Mirrors, 13, 23
Mistletoe, 35
Moon, new, 17

Narcissus legend, 23
Natural History (Pliny), 29

Oates, Johnny, 9
Opening an umbrella indoors, 57
Owls, 31
Ozark mountains, 37

Palmer, Jim, 8
Persians, 19
Photographs, 13
Picture, falling of, 13
Playing cards, throwing overboard, 43

Pliny, 29, 35
Poe, Edgar Allan, 59
Putting on left shoe first, 55

Queen Elizabeth, 23

Raven, 59
Right-left superstitions, 55
Romans, 39, 59
Rime of the Ancient Mariner
    (Coleridge), 47

Sailing superstitions, 43, 47, 57
St. Dunstan, 51
Salt, 39
Scandinavia, 41, 45
Scarecrow, 41
Scotland, 31, 49
Seeing the new moon, 17
Shoes, 21, 55
Shooting an albatross, 47
Sneezing, 15
South African War, 27
Spiders and spider webs, 37
Spilling of salt, 39
"Stealing souls," with photographs,
    13

Stockings, weddings and, 21
Stumbling, 25
Superstition, 8–9
Swedes, 53
"Swedish Match King," 27
Sympathetic magic, 13

Tahitians, 37
Theater superstitions, 25, 43, 45
Thirteen, 45
Thor, 41
Threshold, carrying bride across, 25

Umbrellas, 57
United States, 37, 39

Venetians, 23

Wales, 53
Walking under a ladder, 11
Wedding superstitions, 21, 25
Whistling, 43
White heather, 49
Wind, whistling up, 43
Wishes, made on new moon, 17
World War I, 27

Further Reading

Aylesworth, Thomas G. *Animal Superstitions.* New York: McGraw-Hill, 1981.

Cavendish, Richard, ed. *Mythology: The Illustrated Encyclopedia.* New York: Rizzoli, 1980.

Cohen, Daniel. *Superstition.* Minnesota: Creative Education Press, 1971.

DeFelice, Cynthia. *Willy's Silly Grandma.* New York: Orchard Books, 1997.

Delton, Judy. *It Happened on Thursday.* Chicago: Albert Whitman, 1978.

Grimal, Pierre. *The Dictionary of Classical Mythology.* London: Basil Blackwell, 1986.

Guiley, Rosemary Ellen. *The Encyclopedia of Witches and Witchcraft.* New York: Facts on File, 1989.

Heaps, Willard A. *Superstition!* Nashville: Thomas Nelson, 1972.

Perl, Lila. *Don't Sing Before Breakfast, Don't Sleep in the Moonlight: Everyday Superstitions and How They Began.* New York: Clarion Books, 1988.

Ziefert, Harriet. *Good Luck Bad Luck.* New York: Viking Penguin, 1991.